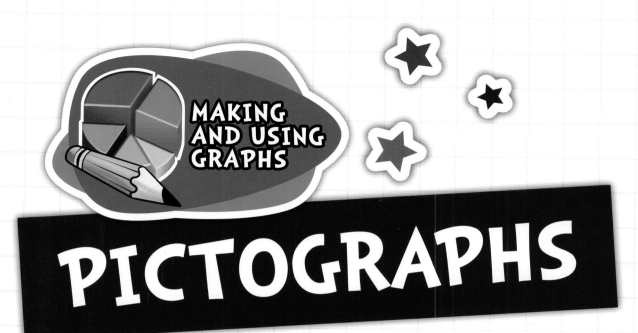

MAKING AND USING GRAPHS

PICTOGRAPHS

by Lisa Colozza Cocca   illustrated by Kathleen Petelinsek

Published in the United States of America by Cherry Lake Publishing
Ann Arbor, Michigan
www.cherrylakepublishing.com

Consultants: Janice Bradley, PhD, Mathematically Connected Communities, New Mexico State University; Marla Conn, Read-Ability

Editorial direction: Rebecca Rowell
Book design and illustration: The Design Lab

Photo credits: Judy Kennamer/Shutterstock Images, 4; Dmitriy Shironosov/Shutterstock Images, 8; Shutterstock Images, 20

Library of Congress Cataloging-in-Publication Data
Cocca, Lisa Colozza, 1957–
  Pictographs / Lisa Colozza Cocca.
      pages cm. — (Making and using graphs)
  Includes bibliographical references and index.
  Audience: Ages 5–7.
  Audience: Grades K to 3.
  ISBN 978-1-61080-913-9 (hardback : alk. paper) – ISBN 978-1-61080-938-2 (paperback : alk. paper) – ISBN 978-1-61080-963-4 (ebook) – ISBN 978-1-61080-988-7 (hosted ebook)
  1. Charts, diagrams, etc.–Juvenile literature. 2. Mathematical statistics–Graphic methods–Juvenile literature. 3. Pictures–Juvenile literature. I. Title.

  QA276.13.C628 2013
  001.4'226–dc23

                          2012032954

0850

Cherry Lake Publishing would like to acknowledge the work of The Partnership for 21st Century Skills. Please visit www.21stcenturyskills.org for more information.

Printed in the United States of America
Corporate Graphics Inc.
January 2013
CLFA10

Table of Contents

CHAPTER ONE

What Is a Pictograph?

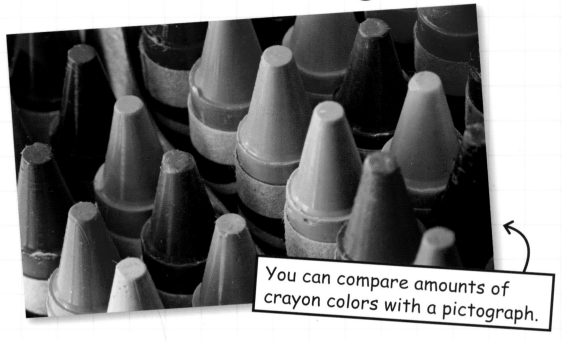

You can compare amounts of crayon colors with a pictograph.

Do you ever have to count and compare things? A pictograph can help. It's a kind of number picture. If you want to compare the numbers of blue crayons and green crayons, a pictograph can help. You can compare other colors, too!

Pictographs can also show how things change over time. A pictograph can show how many pencils you've used during the school year.

Pictographs are easy to read and fun to make. You'll see. Let's get started!

A pictograph has many parts:

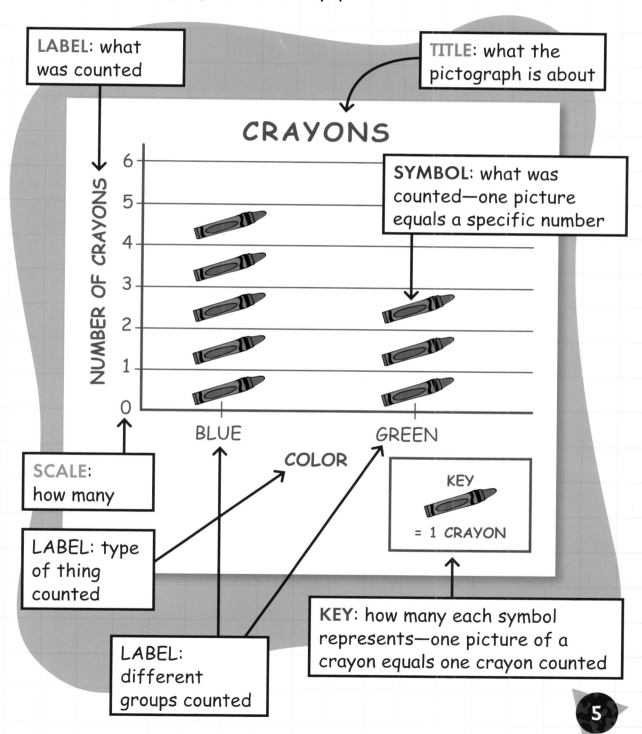

LABEL: what was counted

TITLE: what the pictograph is about

CRAYONS

SYMBOL: what was counted—one picture equals a specific number

NUMBER OF CRAYONS

6
5
4
3
2
1
0

BLUE

GREEN

COLOR

SCALE: how many

LABEL: type of thing counted

LABEL: different groups counted

KEY

= 1 CRAYON

KEY: how many each symbol represents—one picture of a crayon equals one crayon counted

Pictographs use a symbol to show what was counted. The symbol might be a star or a triangle.

A pictograph uses a symbol, or picture, to represent each type of thing counted and to show how many were counted. We arrange the symbols in lines to show data, or information. The lines can be vertical and go from bottom to top. Or the lines can be horizontal and go from side to side. The key tells us how many things each picture stands for.

What kinds of things can we compare in a pictograph? Let's find out!

Here's what you'll need to complete the activities in this book:

- notebook paper
- pencil with an eraser
- ruler
- crayons or markers

Gather what you need.

CHAPTER TWO

Graphing Number of Books Read

A tally chart can help you track a reading contest.

Our school is having a reading contest. The class that reads the most books each month will win a prize. Let's track the number of books read this month by the classes in our grade.

First, we can make a **tally chart**. To tally is to count. Use a tally chart to track what you count. This is a great way to collect data for our graph.

BOOKS READ		
CLASS	NUMBER	TOTAL
Mr. Larsen	ЖЖ ЖЖ |||	13
Miss Velasquez	ЖЖ ЖЖ ЖЖ	15
Mrs. Collins	ЖЖ |||	8
Mr. Hu	ЖЖ ||	7

We made a tally mark for each book read.

Classroom teachers are listed in the left **column**. Each class has its own **row**. We make a **tally mark**, or line, for each book a student in the class reads. The fifth mark goes across the other four.

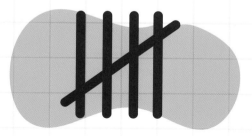

Next, we count the tally marks in each row. We write the total for each class in the chart. The totals go in the right column.

Let's make a vertical pictograph. The teachers' names go across the bottom. Each class will have a column. We write the numbers along the left side. We'll represent each book read with a book symbol. We put that in the key so others will know how to read our pictograph.

Which class read the most books? Which class was second? How many fewer books did the second-place class read than the top class?

Graph Birds

Practice making a pictograph. Compare the colors of birds you see.

INSTRUCTIONS:

1. Use the tally chart on page 9 as a model for your chart.
2. Pick a place to look for birds. Count the different colors of birds you see in one hour.
3. Make a vertical pictograph with your data. If you want, you can use your ruler to make straight lines.
4. Make a column for each color of bird: black, brown, red, blue, and yellow. Draw a bird for each bird you saw.
5. Label the parts of your graph. Remember, the numbers go along the side. The bird colors go along the bottom.
6. Give your graph a title.
7. Make a key so others will know how to read your pictograph.
8. What color bird did you see the most? What color did you see the least?
9. Show a parent your pictograph and explain what it shows.

To get a copy of this activity, visit www.cherrylakepublishing.com/activities.

CHAPTER THREE

Graphing Types of Books

Let's graph the types of books we're reading!

Let's look at books another way. Which kinds of books are students in our class reading? There are many types to choose from. Some kids like to read sports stories. Others like to read animal or superhero stories. Let's see which types of books are most popular. We'll focus on our class.

We collected our data in a tally chart. It shows how many of each type of book our class is reading right now. Let's make a pictograph using this data.

BOOKS OUR CLASS IS READING		
TYPE OF BOOK	NUMBER	TOTAL
Sports	ⵏⵏⵏ	5
Animal	||||	4
History	|	1
Biography	||	2
Mystery	|||	3
Science Fiction	ⵏⵏⵏ |	6

Kids are reading lots of different books.

Super Monkey Saves the Day!

Let's make a horizontal pictograph. The types of books go along the side. The numbers go along the bottom. The key shows that one star equals one book being read.

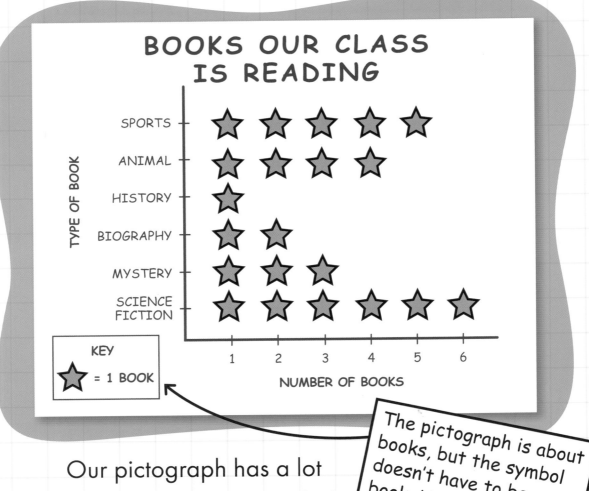

BOOKS OUR CLASS IS READING

KEY

☆ = 1 BOOK

The pictograph is about books, but the symbol doesn't have to be a book. Here, one star stands for one book.

Our pictograph has a lot of information. Which kind of book is most popular in our class right now? Which is least popular?

Graph Hair Color

Make a pictograph to compare the hair color of people you see.

INSTRUCTIONS:
1. Use the tally chart on page 13 as a model.
2. Count the number of people you see by hair color: black, brown, red, blond. You can include no hair, too. The people can be classmates, family, friends, or strangers walking by.
3. Make a horizontal pictograph with your data. If you want, use your ruler to make straight lines.
4. Put your data in rows. Draw a face for each person you counted.
5. Label the parts of your graph. Remember, things counted go along the side. The numbers go along the bottom.
6. Give your graph a title.
7. Make a key.
8. Which hair color did you see most? Did you see and graph any colors not listed above?
9. Tell a friend what your pictograph shows.

To get a copy of this activity, visit www.cherrylakepublishing.com/activities.

CHAPTER FOUR

Graphing Books Read Over Time

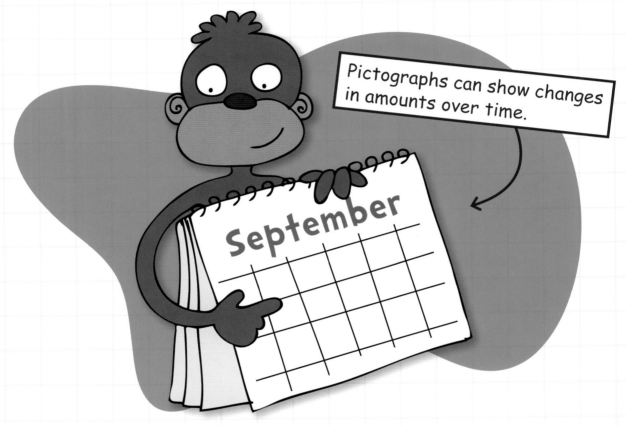

Pictographs can show changes in amounts over time.

A few months have passed since we started the reading contest. Let's see how many books our class has read. This is another way we can study our data. We look at how something changes over time. In this case, it's the number of books we read from month to month.

First, let's gather our data in a chart.

BOOKS OUR CLASS HAS READ	
MONTH	TOTAL
September	12
October	16
November	20
December	13
January	22

Here's our data. Let's graph it!

The months our class has been in the reading contest are on the left side. The number of books our class read each month is on the right. This time, instead of using tally marks, we just use numbers.

Let's graph our data in a vertical pictograph. The months go across the bottom. The number of books read goes along the side. This time, each symbol will be worth more than one. Each picture will equal two books.

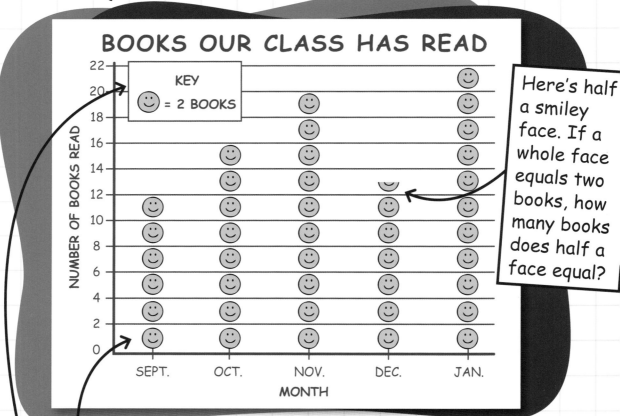

BOOKS OUR CLASS HAS READ

KEY

☺ = 2 BOOKS

NUMBER OF BOOKS READ

MONTH

Here's half a smiley face. If a whole face equals two books, how many books does half a face equal?

Smiley faces represent books read. Each face equals two books.

Can you read the graph? How many books did our class read in September? How many more books did we read in January than in December?

Graph Lemonade Sales

Practice graphing data to show change over time. Pretend you have a lemonade stand. Graph your lemonade sales to see which day had the most sales.

INSTRUCTIONS:
1. Make a vertical pictograph to show how much lemonade you sold.
2. Make three columns: Friday, Saturday, and Sunday.
3. Write the title: Lemonade Sales.
4. Make your key. One symbol of your choice equals two cups of lemonade sold.
5. Add the data to your graph. On Friday, you sold 10 cups of lemonade. Draw your symbol five times to show this. On Saturday, you sold 14 cups. On Sunday, you sold six cups.
6. Which day had the most sales? Which day had the least?
7. Tell a teacher what your pictograph shows.

To get a copy of this activity, visit www.cherrylakepublishing.com/activities.

CHAPTER FIVE

Pictographs Are Fun

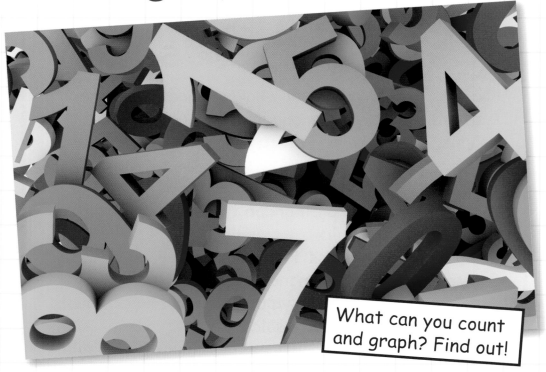

What can you count and graph? Find out!

Pictographs are an easy way to share information. They're also fun to make. Pictographs show data using pictures. We can use pictographs to compare amounts of things. We can see how something changes over time, too.

You've seen how pictographs can tell you about crayons, books, bird color, hair color, and lemonade sales. What else can you show in a pictograph? Start counting and find out!

Here are other fun ways you can use a pictograph:

- Study your friends and family by eye color.
- Compare the sports your friends like to play.
- Count the number of calls to your home telephone each day for one week. Show how the number changes from day to day.
- Help with the dishes. Compare the number of plates, cups, and bowls you wash or dry.

You can show amounts of all kinds of things with pictographs, including dishes.

Glossary

column (KAH-luhm) a vertical line of data

data (DAY-tuh) information recorded about people or things

horizontal (hor-i-ZAHN-tuhl) going straight across or side to side

key (kee) a list or chart that tells what the pictures or symbols in a graph stand for

label (LAY-buhl) a name; to give something a name

row (roh) a horizontal line of data

scale (skale) a series of numbers that shows how many

symbol (SIM-buhl) a picture that stands for something else

tally chart (TAL-ee chahrt) a way to record things you count that uses tally marks

tally mark (TAL-ee mahrk) a line that stands for one item of something being counted

title (TYE-tuhl) the name of a chart

vertical (VUR-ti-kuhl) going straight up and down

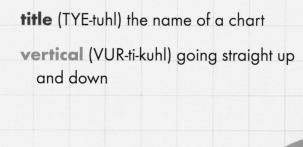

For More Information

BOOKS

Bodach, Vijaya Khisty. *Pictographs.* Mankato, MN: Capstone, 2008.

Cortland, D. J. *A Week of Weather: Learning to Collect and Record Data on a Pictograph.* New York: Rosen, 2004.

Trumbauer, Lisa. *Graph It!* Mankato, MN: Yellow Umbrella, 2002.

WEB SITES

Beacon Learning Center—I Am Special!
www.beaconlearningcenter.com/WebLessons/IAmSpecial/me01.htm
Learn about what makes Rebecca special by reading pictographs about Rebecca and her friends.

SoftSchools.com—Make Your Own Pictograph
www.softschools.com/math/data_analysis/pictograph/make_your_own_pictograph/
Build a pictograph online with this fun tool.

SoftSchools.com—Pictograph Game
www.softschools.com/math/data_analysis/pictograph/games/
Answer the questions using the pictographs in this online game.

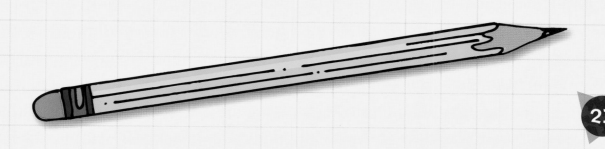

Index

About the Author

Lisa Colozza Cocca is a former teacher and school librarian. For the past decade, she has worked as a freelance writer and editor. She lives, works, and plays in New Jersey. Lisa thinks graphs are lots of fun.